Wings of Destiny

The Remarkable Life and Legacy of Eric Brown, Britain's Greatest Test Pilot

Olivier Scoffield

Table Of Contents

Preface

Captain Eric Melrose "Winkle" Brown, CBE, DSC, AFC, Hon FRAeS was a British Royal Navy officer and test pilot who flew 487 different types of aircraft, more than any other person in history.

Brown set several "firsts" in naval aviation, including the first landings of a twin-engined aircraft, an aircraft with a tricycle undercarriage, a jet aircraft, and a rotary-wing aircraft on an aircraft carrier (2,407 and 2,271 respectively). Brown also holds the world record for the most aircraft carrier deck takeoffs and landings performed.

Brown piloted nearly all types of Royal Navy and Royal Air Force aircraft, including helicopters, flying boats, fighters, bombers, airliners, amphibians, and gliders. He piloted a wide variety of seized German, Italian, and Japanese aircraft during World War II, including brand-new jet and rocket planes. In the postwar era, he was a pioneer of jet technology.

EARLY YEARS

In the United Kingdom's Leith, close to
Edinburgh, Brown was born, on the 21st of
January 1919. When Brown was eight or ten
years old, his father, a former balloon observer
and pilot in the Royal Flying Corps (RFC) took
him up in a Gloster Gauntlet as the younger
Brown sat on his father's knee.

Brown's father accompanied him to the 1936
Berlin Olympics. After Hermann Göring
revealed the existence of the Luftwaffe,
members of the group contacted Brown and his
father and extended invitations to attend social

events. At one of these gatherings, retired First World War fighter ace Ernst Udet struck up a conversation with former RFC pilot Brown Sr. and volunteered to introduce Eric to flying. After arriving at the designated airstrip in Halle, Eric immediately accepted the German's offer, and he was soon flying in a two-seat Bücker Jungmann. He discussed the incident on the BBC radio show Desert Island Discs nearly 80 years later.

You mention aerobatics; I believe we performed each one while I was holding onto my stomach. As I exited the cockpit, he slapped me between the shoulder blades and gave me the old WW1 fighter pilots'

greeting, Hals- und Beinbruch, which translates to "broken neck and broken legs," but that was their salutation. He had given me the scare of my life as we approached upside-down and then he rolled out just in time to land. However, he told me that I would become a good fighter pilot if I learned to speak German well and learned to fly.

After graduating from the Royal High School in 1937, Brown enrolled in the University of Edinburgh to study modern languages, with a focus on German. He joined the school's air unit while there and began receiving formal flying instruction.

After receiving an invitation from Udet, who was then a major general in the Luftwaffe, to attend the 1938 Automobile Exhibition, he went to Germany under the patronage of the Foreign Office in February 1938. He witnessed Hanna Reitsch's display of the Focke-Wulf Fw 61 helicopter in front of a small audience in the Deutschlandhalle. He met and came to know Reitsch during this tour; they had previously just spoken in passing in 1936.

In the interim, Brown had been chosen to participate as an exchange student at the Schule Schloss Salem, which is situated on the shores of Lake Constance. It was while Brown was studying abroad in Germany in September 1939 that Brown was startled awake by a loud tapping at his door. He was greeted by a woman who said "Our countries are at war" as he opened the door. Brown was taken into custody by the SS shortly after. After holding him for three days, they simply led Brown over the Swiss border in his MG Magnette sports car, telling him they were letting him retain the vehicle since they "had no spares for it."

MILITARY SERVICE

He joined the Royal Air Force Volunteer
Reserve upon his return to the war-torn United
Kingdom before switching to the Royal Navy
Volunteer Reserve as a Fleet Air Arm pilot. He
was assigned to the 802 Naval Air Squadron and
began his service on the first escort carrier,
HMS Audacity, which was converted and given
that name in July 1941. He piloted a Grumman
Martlet from the carrier. Using head-on attacks
to take advantage of the blind hole in their
defensive weaponry, he shot down two Focke-
Wulf Fw 200 Condor maritime patrol aircraft
when he was serving on board Audacity.

On December 21, 1941, the German submarine U-751, under the leadership of Gerhard Bigalk, torpedoed and sank Audacity. Due to concerns about a nearby U-boat, the first rescue ship departed, leaving Brown and a small group of survivors in the sea overnight until they were found the following day. Of the 24 people, he was the only one to avoid hypothermia; the others perished from exposure to the cold. 407 out of the total 480 people survived.

The death toll was so great that the 802 Squadron wasn't reconstituted until February 1942. In particular, Brown received the

Distinguished Service Cross "For bravery and skill in action against Enemy aircraft and in the protection of a Convoy against heavy and sustained Enemy attacks" for his work on the Audacity on March 10, 1942.

After Audacity went down, Brown resumed active flying and was seconded to RCAF squadrons to fly escort missions with USAAF Boeing B-17 Flying Fortress bombers over France. Although the training was done on airfields, it was his responsibility to instruct them in deck-landing procedures. He took part in their fighter missions as a form of payment in exchange.

In 1943, he was operational once more and returned to the Royal Aeronautical Establishment (RAE) to conduct experimental flying. He even batted in the much more seasoned Admiralty Test Pilot Lieutenant Commander Roy Sydney Baker-Falkner to fly the experimental Fairey Barracuda onto the deck of a carrier in the Clyde. He was moved to Southern Italy almost immediately to assess seized Regia Aeronautica and Luftwaffe planes. Brown accomplished this with essentially little tuition, using the information that could be found in the available sources. After he had finished these tasks, his commander, who had been pleased with his performance, recommended that he be hired by Farnborough's Aerodynamics Flight department and sent him back to the RAE. Brown flew 13 different types of aircraft during his first month with the Flight, among them a captured Focke-Wulf Fw 190.

To use Brown's expertise in deck landings, the Royal Aircraft Establishment (RAE) at Farnborough posted him there. He initially tested the newly navalized Sea Hurricane and Seafire when he was there. His skill with deck landings led to his appointment to a position evaluating carriers' landing systems before they entered into service. By the end of 1943, he had completed around 1,500 deck landings on 22 different carriers as a consequence of the testing, which encompassed numerous permutations of the landing spot and type of aircraft. Brown noted that he hardly ever took any time off throughout his six years at RAE. On September 9, 1943, while conducting carrier compatibility tests, Brown crashed-landed a Fairey Firefly Mk I, Z1844, on the deck of HMS Pretoria Castle because the batsman failed to notice that the arrestor hook was not in the "down" position and the arrestor hook indicator light misled him into believing it was. The fighter struck the crash barrier, tearing off the vehicle's undercarriage and propeller, but he sustained no injuries.

Brown participated in the deck landing trials of the de Havilland Sea Mosquito, the heaviest aircraft yet chosen to be flown from a British carrier while serving as the chief navy test pilot at Farnborough. On March 25, 1944, Brown made his first landing on HMS Indefatigable. This was a twin-engined aircraft's first landing on a ship. The aircraft's stall speed was 110 knots (200 km/h; 130 mph), whereas the fastest speed for a deck landing was 86 knots (159 km/h; 99 mph).

Additionally, he flew multiple tours with Fighter Command in Great Britain's air defense.

In the summer of 1944, a V-1 "Doodlebug" cruise missile demolished Brown's house, concussing his wife and seriously hurting their housekeeper.

Brown got involved in this kind of test, which was flown where the aircraft, typically a Supermarine Spitfire, would be dived at speeds of the high subsonic and near the transonic area. At the time, the RAE was the leading authority on high-speed flight. During these tests, Squadron Leader Anthony F. Martindale and Brown were able to achieve speeds of Mach

0.86 in a conventional Spitfire MK IX and Mach

0.92 in a modified Spitfire PR Mk XI.

Supporting The Eighth Air Force Of The USAAF

The RAE Aerodynamics Flight also comprised two other test pilots, Sqn Ldrs. James "Jimmy" Nelson and Douglas Weightman, in addition to Brown and Martindale. The 8th Air Force was having trouble when their Lockheed P-38 Lightning, Republic P-47 Thunderbolt, and North American P-51 Mustang fighters, providing top cover for the bombers, dove down onto attacking German fighters, with some of the diving U.S. fighters encountering speed regions where they became difficult to control. During this time, USAAF General Jimmy

Doolittle approached the RAE with a request for assistance.

Early in 1944, Brown and many other pilots drove the P-38H Lightning, a Packard Merlin-powered P-51B Mustang, and a P-47C Thunderbolt for compressibility tests at the RAE at Doolittle's request. According to the test results, the tactical Mach values, or maneuvering limitations, for the Lightning and Thunderbolt were Mach 0.68 and Mach 0.71, respectively; the corresponding figure for the Fw 190 and Messerschmitt Bf 109 was Mach 0.75, giving them the advantage in a dive. Nevertheless, Doolittle was able to convince his superiors to choose the Mustang over the P-38 and P-47 for all escort duties going forward because those aircraft were becoming more common by very early 1944. This led to Doolittle's eventual transition to air supremacy missions, which allowed the fighters to fly up to 75–100 miles ahead of the bomber combat box formations, inst.

First Experiences With Jet Travel

After making a flight diversion to RAF
Cranwell due to bad weather in May 1941,
Brown learned about the British advancements
in jet propulsion. He later met Frank Whittle
when he was asked to suggest modifications to
the jet engine to make it more suitable for naval
use. The Gloster Meteor was chosen as the
Royal Navy's first jet fighter as a result,
however, few would be utilized by them. Brown
was also chosen to fly the Miles M.52
supersonic research aircraft, and he did so
while piloting modified aircraft fitted with
M.52-related parts. However, the post-war

administration terminated the project in 1945, just as the M.52 was nearing completion. He received the Order of the British Empire's designation as a Member on May 2, 1944, "for outstanding enterprise and skill in piloting aircraft during hazardous aircraft trials."

Brown discovered that the Aerodynamics Flight had been given three Sikorsky R-4B Hoverfly/Gadfly helicopters in February 1945. Brown enjoyed a brief flight as a passenger in one of these tail-rotor aircraft when a trip to Farnborough was organized because he had never seen one. A few days later, RAF Speke

dispatched Brown and Martindale to pick up
two fresh R-4Bs.

When they arrived, they discovered the
American mechanics putting the machines
together. When Brown inquired about
Martindale and himself receiving training to fly
the aircraft, the Master Sergeant in charge
handed him a "big orange-colored booklet" and
responded, "Whaddya mean, bud? Here is your
teacher. Following a few practice hovering and
controlling the craft attempts and a hard drink,
Brown and Martindale reviewed the guidebook
before leaving for Farnborough. Brown and
Martindale navigated the journey successfully,

if sloppily, in formation, despite occasionally being several miles apart.

While participating in trials for the flexible deck concept with HMS Pretoria Castle on April 4, Brown added another "first" to his record book. He was required to make several landing approaches to the escort carrier in a Bell Airacobra that had, coincidentally, been modified with a tail hook. A deck landing was permitted when Brown declared an emergency during one of these passes, as had been previously agreed upon with the carrier's commander, Caspar John. Although the landing was effortless, there was little room for error even with the ship steaming at full speed due to the Airacobra's lengthy takeoff run. This was the aircraft's first carrier landing and takeoff with a tricycle undercarriage.

The RAE's "Enemy Flight"

Brown was appointed the commanding officer of "Operation Enemy Flight" as the end of the European War drew near. The RAE was preparing to acquire German aeronautical technology and aircraft before they were either accidentally destroyed or taken by the Soviets. He took off for northern Germany, where the Arado Ar 234, a brand-new jet bomber that the Allies, especially the Americans, were greatly interested in, was one of the targets for the RAE. Since the German army had fled to Denmark, a number of the planes were stationed there. He anticipated reaching a liberated aerodrome shortly after the British Army had taken it, but due to German opposition to the Allied advance, the ground forces were delayed and the airfield was still being used as a Luftwaffe base. Fortunately for Brown, the Luftwaffe airfield commanding officer at Grove accepted his surrender, and Brown seized control of the airfield and its 2,000 staff members until Allied forces arrived the following day.

Later, Brown and Martindale transported twelve Ar 234s across the North Sea and on to Farnborough with the help of a cooperative German pilot and several other members of the

Aerodynamics Flight. It was a risky undertaking because Brown and his colleagues had no idea how many engine hours the aircraft was estimated to have left. After all, the Germans had burned all of the engine log books before they were captured. The Junkers Jumo 004 engines had a life of only 25 hours due to the dearth of the specialized high-temperature alloys used in their manufacturing; it was therefore unknown whether the engines were fresh or just about to run out of fuel.

Brown was invited to assist in questioning the former camp commandant and his aide during this time by Brigadier Glyn Hughes, the medical officer of the British Second Army occupying the recently liberated Bergen-Belsen concentration camp. Irma Grese and Josef Kramer were interrogated shortly after he agreed to do so, and he later said of the experience, "Two more loathsome creatures it is hard to imagine," calling the latter "... the worst human being I have ever met." After being found guilty of war crimes, Kramer and Grese were executed.

Postwar

Brown oversaw the Enemy Aircraft Flight, a select squad of pilots that tested seized German and Italian aircraft after the Second World War. Brown was among the few personnel who were qualified to assess both Allied and Axis aircraft as they flew during the war thanks to his experience. 53 German aircraft, including the Messerschmitt Me 163 Komet rocket fighter, were tested in flight by him. The National Museum of Flight in the United Kingdom, located east of Edinburgh, presently houses that Komet.

His unofficial flying test of this rocket plane—
the only one by an Allied pilot employing the
rocket motor—was completed because the
notoriously risky C-Stoff fuel and T-Stoff
oxidizer combination made it more or less
suicidal.

In a September 2015 interview with a
newspaper, he recalled,

**It was a brand-new experience for me and
the most thrilling thing I could imagine.
Before takeoff, I distinctly recall closely
observing the ground crew and speculating
as to whether they believed they were
saying goodbye to me for real or that this
monster would eventually return. It created**

an enormously thundering sound, and
because everything was changing so quickly,
it was like being in charge of a runaway
train. I had to be extremely alert.

All three of the German jet prototypes that saw
front-line combat during the war—the
Messerschmitt Me 262A Schwalbe, the Arado
Ar 234B Blitz, each powered by twin Junkers
Jumo 004 engines, and the Heinkel He 162A
Spatz turbojet combat aircraft—were flight-
tested by Brown. Later, when he flew the He
162A at the Farnborough Air Show, he said that
it had the best controls of any aircraft he had
ever flown but was also challenging to control.

At Farnborough, one of his coworkers perished while testing the aircraft type.

As a German native speaker following World War II, Brown assisted in interviewing several Germans, including Wernher von Braun, Hermann Göring, Willy Messerschmitt, Ernst Heinkel, and Kurt Tank. The Nuremberg proceedings had to get underway, therefore he said the interviews were brief and only covered aviation-related topics.

The RAE Flight, headquartered at the former Luftwaffe airfield in Schleswig, was utilizing a specially modified Focke-Wulf Fw 200 Condor that had been captured and belonged to Himmler. Brown was flying this aircraft. Additionally, he was able to reconnect with German pilot Hanna Reitsch, whom he had first met in Germany before the war. After the Germans submitted in 1945, she was detained. Her father had slain her mother, sister, and himself out of fear of the approaching Russians.

He participated in the Miles M.52 supersonic project during World War II as an RAE test pilot, flying a Spitfire equipped with the M.52's all-moving tail and diving from great heights to reach extremely high subsonic speeds. In 1946, he was scheduled to fly the M.52, but when the project was abandoned, this didn't happen. Chuck Yeager became the first person to surpass Mach 1 in 1947 thanks to Bell's modification of its XS-1 for true transonic pitch controllability, which was made possible by the British government's request for the information about all moving tails (although no information was ever received in return).

Brown would have been the front-runner for the Megaroc sub-orbital manned spacecraft's anticipated 1949 debut flight had the Ministry of Supply moved forward with Ralph Smith's V2-based design.

Brown undertook comparable testing of the Avro Tudor airliner while at the RAE, harkening back to his days testing aircraft in high-speed dives. To prepare for a future four-jet Tudor version, it was necessary to ascertain the safe limiting speed for the aircraft and collect information on large civil aircraft's high-speed handling. He succeeded in diving the Tudor up to Mach 0.7 while flying from 32,000 feet, an unusual speed for such a large piston-engined aircraft. This speed was determined at the pilot's discretion because pulling the aircraft out of the dive had required the combined efforts of Brown and his second pilot. The Tudor, however, was a failure as an airliner. The Avro Ashton would eventually replace the Tudor's intended jet variant.

After Geoffrey de Havilland, Jr. was killed in a crash in a comparable aircraft while diving at speeds close to the sound barrier, he test-flew a modified (strengthened and control-boosted) de Havilland DH.108 in 1949. Brown began his experiments at a height of 35,000 feet and eventually reached 45,000 feet, where he dived and attained a Mach number of 0.985. He didn't realize the aircraft had a high-g pitch oscillation at many hertz (Hz) in a Mach 0.88 descent from that altitude until he tried the experiments from the same height as de Havilland, at 4,000 ft.

The ride was smooth, and then all of a sudden it fell apart... as the plane porpoised wildly, my chin hit my chest, I jerked hardback, slammed forward again, and repeated it over and over, feeling like I was being flogged by the awful whipping of the plane.

Brown was able to gently draw back on the stick and throttle by recalling the practice he had frequently rehearsed, and the action "... ceased as quickly as it had started." De Havilland fractured his neck during the test flight, possibly as a result of the extreme oscillation, so he thought that part of the reason he survived the mission was because he was a shorter guy.

Test equipment on Brown's flight captured data during oscillations at +4 and 3 g's at 3 Hz. The DH 108, according to Brown, is "a killer nasty stall, dreadful, unabated longitudinal oscillation in bumps. The three DH 108 aircraft were all destroyed in tragic mishaps.

Brown received the Boyd Trophy in 1948 for his efforts in the rubber deck landing system experiments. On March 30, 1949, he received a permanent commission in the Royal Navy as a lieutenant, with seniority retroactive to his initial advancement to the rank during the war.

He was testing Saunders-Roe SR.A/1 TG271, the third of three jet-powered flying-boat fighter prototypes, on August 12, 1949, when he collided with underwater debris, causing the aircraft to drown in the Solent off Cowes, Isle of Wight. His Saunders-Roe test pilot Geoffrey Tyson retrieved him from the destroyed plane after he had been knocked out in the collision. On April 1, 1951, he was promoted to lieutenant commander, then to commander on December 31, 1953, and finally to captain on December 31, 1960.

At least three significant firsts in carrier aviation can be attributed to Brown: the first carrier landing using an aircraft equipped with a tricycle undercarriage (the Bell Airacobra Mk 1 AH574) on the trials carrier HMS Pretoria Castle on April 4, 1945; the first landing of a twin-engined aircraft (the Mosquito) on a carrier (HMS Indefatigable (R10) on March 25, 1944; and the first carrier landing of a jet aircraft, the de He eventually received the title of Officer of the Order of the British Empire in recognition of his efforts with the Mosquito and the Vampire.

Brown flew a variety of American aircraft, including 36 different models of helicopters, while stationed at the Naval Air Station Patuxent River in Maryland for two years as an exchange officer during the Korean War in the 1950s. At Patuxent River in January 1952, Brown gave Americans a demonstration of the steam catapult by launching a Grumman Panther while the carrier HMS Perseus was still docked at the Philadelphia Naval Yard. As the new steam catapult was capable of launching an aircraft into the air without any wind, British officials decided that they would risk their pilot (Brown) if the Americans would risk their aircraft. It had been planned for Brown to make the first catapult launch with the ship underway and steaming into any wind. The steam catapult would eventually be used by US carriers since the launch was successful.

Around the same time, Brown was once again asked to promote the idea of the angled flight deck, another British technology that was being given to the US. Whether or not it was because of Brown, USS Antietam, the first US aircraft carrier outfitted with the new flight deck, was ready in less than nine months.

Brown, who was by this time a Commander in the Royal Navy, was appointed Commander

(Air) of RNAS Brawdy in 1954. He held this position until late 1957 when he returned to Germany and assumed the position of Chief of the British Naval Mission to Germany. His task was to restore German naval aviation following its pre-war integration with and subservience to the Luftwaffe. Brown collaborated closely with Admiral Gerhard Wagner of the German Naval Staff during this time. Brown was given a personal Percival Pembroke aircraft by the Marineflieger during this time, which, to his surprise, the German maintenance staff took great pride in. The training was initially undertaken in the UK on Hawker Sea Hawks and Fairey Gannets during this time. In actuality, it was the German Navy's first entirely naval aircraft since the 1930s. Brown oversaw the resurgence of naval aviation in Germany, and as a result, Marineflieger squadrons joined NATO in 1960.

After the business's previous test pilot was arrested because he had family in East Germany, Brown enjoyed a brief three-month stint as a test pilot for the Focke-Wulf company. He assisted them while they searched for a successor.

Brown was consulted on the flight deck layout of the projected new UK class of aircraft carrier, the CVA-01, in the 1960s due to his extensive knowledge in carrier aviation while serving as the Admiralty's deputy director of Naval Air Warfare, even though the project was abandoned in 1966.

His final position in the Royal Navy came in September 1967 when, as a captain, he assumed command of HMS Fulmar. From March 1970 to 1972, he was in charge of the Royal Naval Air Station in Lossiemouth. On July 7, 1969, he was chosen to serve as Queen Elizabeth II's naval aide de camp, and in the 1970 New Year Honors, he was named a Commander of the Order of the British Empire. On January 27,

1970, he gave up his position as naval ADC, and he retired from the Royal Navy later that year.

LATER YEARS

From 1982 to 1983, Brown presided over the Royal Aeronautical Society. Although he made his last flight as a pilot in 1994, in 2015 he was still giving lectures and frequently attends the British Rocketry Oral History Programme (BROHP), where the Sir Arthur Clarke Awards are presented each year. He received their Lifetime Achievement Award in 2007.

Brown resided in Copthorne, West Sussex, where he was semi-retired. In 1942, he wed Evelyn (Lynn) Macrory. 1998 saw her passing. He was interviewed numerous times, most recently in April 2013 at his house by BBC Radio 4.

The hour-long BBC Two documentary Britain's Greatest Pilot: The Extraordinary Story of Captain Winkle Brown was about him in June 2014. Mark Bowman, the chief test pilot of BAE Systems, commented on those accomplishments, "They didn't have the advantage of high-tech simulators. He would have been piloting the aircraft with "the benefit of a slide rule, not a bank of computers as we have now," the author continued. He simply had to look at the aircraft and consider what he was going to do with it.

He was the special guest on the 3,000th episode of BBC Radio 4's Desert Island Discs in November 2014. The 95-year-old stated he still enjoyed driving and had recently purchased a new sports car during the program. He chose "At Last" by the Glenn Miller Orchestra and "Amazing Grace" by the Royal Scots Dragoon Guards as his musical selections. Artie Shaw and His Orchestra's "Stardust" was his favorite song.

"Britain's Defence shortly" was the topic of Brown's Mountbatten Lecture at the University of Edinburgh on February 24, 2015. He cautioned: "The Russians are playing a very dangerous game of chess," while speaking at the Playfair Library. "They are fully engaged in the game. It might turn out like that. There is no doubt that it exhibits the same symptoms as what sparked the Cold War."

Brown received the Founder's Medal from the Air League in May 2015. At the annual ceremony held at St. James's Palace, this was given to him by the patron, the Duke of Edinburgh, "for his amazing flying achievements and involvement with aviation during a remarkable lifetime."

After a brief illness, Brown passed away quietly
on February 21, 2016, at the age of 97, at the
East Surrey Hospital in Redhill, Surrey.

RECORDS

Brown has the record for flying the most different types of aircraft, according to the Guinness Book of World Records, and he has flown aircraft from Britain, the United States, Germany, the Soviet Union, Italy, and Japan. The total number is 487, but it only contains fundamental types. For instance, Brown flew 14 variations of the Spitfire and Seafire, even though these variations are highly distinct from one another. Only aircraft that Brown has operated as "Captain in Command" are included on this list.

Brown believed that this record would never be broken due to the unique conditions involved.

Additionally, during the Second World War, he tested the arrestor wires on more than 20 aircraft carriers, which contributed to his 2,407 carrier landing record.

Credits

Brown mentions several deserving colleagues in his book Wings on My Sleeve that he admires:

I had the good fortune to work with excellent COs including Alan Hards, Dick Ubee, Silyn Roberts, and Allen Wheeler. Meeting and conversing with men like Geoffrey Tyson, Harald Penrose, Jeffrey Quill, Mutt Summers, Bill Pegg, and George Errington about the business of flying was always exciting to me. Geoffrey de Havilland, Bill Humble, and Alex Henshaw were all heroes in my hall of fame before I even knew them. Mike Lithgow, Peter Twiss, John Cunningham of the Comet, John Derry,

Neville Duke, and Roland Beamont were all individuals of extraordinary dynamism.

The names of what Brown refers to as "boffins and boffinettes," include the brilliant aerodynamicists Morien Morgan, Handel Davies, Dai Morris, and P. A. Hufton, as well as the "boffinettes" like aerodynamicist Gwen Alston and structural engineer Anne Burns, are then mentioned. The pilot of the first jet flight in Britain, Gerry Sayer, is also mentioned.

Lewis Boddington, Dr. Thomlinson, John Noble, and Charles Crowfoot are mentioned in Brown's final credits as the individuals credited (together with "others") with "giving the Royal

Navy a technical lead in aircraft carrier

equipment which it still holds to this day 1978."

"These men and women were civil servants, but

they worked long hours, accepted

responsibility, and produced results far beyond

what their country paid them for," he writes as

he concludes this part. "They stand for the real

test of Britain's grandeur, in my opinion."

Books

Brown wrote many books on his adventures, including an autobiography called Wings on My Sleeve which was first published in 1961 and significantly updated in later editions, as well as volumes outlining the flight characteristics of the various aircraft he flew. 'Wings of the Luftwaffe', 'Wings of the Weird and Wonderful', and 'Miles M.52' (co-written with Dennis Bancroft) were further volumes. He also wrote numerous articles for journals and periodicals related to aviation.

His most well-known body of work is the "Viewed from the Cockpit" series of essays, which was printed in the journal Air International and occasionally reprinted. The following categories of flight review highlights have been featured in this series:

- Dornier Do 217
- Fairey Swordfish
- Fairey Fulmar
- Fairey Spearfish, a prototype torpedo bomber (1947) which Brown did not enjoy
- Fairey Barracuda, which Brown found lacklustre and somewhat disappointing
- Focke-Wulf Fw 190 A and D Series.

- Grumman F9F Panther and Grumman F-9 Cougar, which Brown found (on initial models) somewhat underpowered

- Hawker Sea Fury

- Hawker Sea Hurricane

- Heinkel He 111

- Junkers Ju 87D Stuka

- Supermarine Seafire, various marks.

- Messerschmitt Bf 109 E (Emil) and G (Gustav) – Brown flew the G-12 training sub-type from the rear cockpit and nearly crashed because of poor visibility from that position.

- Messerschmitt Me 163 Komet. Brown was one of few pilots to successfully fly one of these, having signed a disclaimer for the German ground crew.

- Messerschmitt Me 262 Schwalbe.
- Heinkel He 177 Greif bomber

Brown explains his preferences as follows:

The de Havilland Hornet is one of my favorites from the (period of piston engines). simply because it was overpowered. This peculiar aspect of an airplane allows you to practically do everything that two engines could achieve. It was a "hot rod Mosquito," and I always compared it to driving a Ferrari through the air.

On the jet side, I was a huge fan of the F-86 Sabre, especially the Model E (F-86E) with the flying tail because it gave me what I like to refer to as the "perfect harmony of control." When a pilot possesses this flawless balance of control, you truly feel like you are a part of the airplane. Once inside, the aircraft greets you with a smile and the words "Thank God you've come, you're part of me anyway." Flying like that is an absolute thrill.

Nickname

Brown was affectionately referred to as "Winkle" by his Royal Navy coworkers. Brown was given the nickname "Periwinkle"— a tiny mollusk—because of his low stature of 5 feet 7 inches (1.70 meters). Brown said that his ability to "curl himself up in the cockpit" helped him survive risky situations.

RECOGNITION AND PRIZES

- 10 March 1942: The Distinguished Service Cross (DSC) is given to HMS Audacity's Temporary Sub-Lieutenant (A) Eric Melrose Brown RNVR "For bravery and skill in action against Enemy aircraft and in the protection of a Convoy against heavy and sustained Enemy attacks."

- 2 May 1944: A member of the Order of the British Empire is named for Temporary Lieutenant (A) Eric Melrose Brown, DSC, RNVR, "for outstanding enterprise and skill in piloting aircraft during hazardous flight trials."

- February 19, 1946: Officer of the Order of the British Empire Eric Melrose Brown, MBE, DSC, RNVR, is appointed temporary acting lieutenant commander (A). For executing the initial deck landings of the Mosquito and Vampire with daring, outstanding skill, and dedication to duty. In doing so, he became the first pilot to ever land a twin-engined (Mosquito) and a solely jet-powered (Vampire) aircraft on the deck of a ship. His outstanding flying ability has played a significant role in the accomplishment of these significant advancements in naval aviation.

- June 6, 1947: The Air Force Cross is given to Lieutenant Commander Eric Brown OBE DSC.

- First day of 1949: The King's Commendation for Valuable Service in the Air was given to Lieutenant Commander E. M. Brown, OBE, DSC, and AFC.

- January 1, 1970: The Royal Navy's Captain Eric Melrose Brown, OBE, DSC, AFC, is made a Commander of the Order of the British Empire on.

- July 3, 2018: Eric Brown's statue was unveiled at Edinburgh Airport..

Printed in Great Britain
by Amazon

34138759R00040